↓ underground books *↓ 1*

Veer _ Robert Kramer

printed in NYC 2018
ISBN: 978-1-7322097-0-1
www.undergroundbooks.org

Veer

By Robert Kramer

For My Daughter Karen

VEER

50 Poems
Robert Kramer

Table of Contents

Acknowledgments

My child in March   Absoloose

High in the hills of the night   Rattapallax

The severed hand   Absoloose

The return   Third Wednesday

Winter night on Central Park West   Glimpse

Upon the spiral staircase of farewells

                                        Poets

The order we have established here

                          Third Wednesday

Like someone not well rehearsed   The Same

P.H. in Paris   Slab

Voices   Absoloose

My child in March

I

As the children's anatomically correct snowman
in his finest suit of soot
slowly dissolves into March,
they run to watch a mongrel mount a splendid setter bitch,
observe him buck and shaft, and study close her eyes.

II

But then alone she ponders
further on the mystery
of those great and moving masses of the air
that we call wind,
invisible and mighty, circling high above the planet,
or howling down a chimney, whistling at a window,
wrenching branches from the trees,
or merely buffeting a solitary child
in the city's barren streets.

III

Vertiginous preoccupations,
at times ferment,
as the child will notice in the carpet
hidden scenes and violent faces,
that – when she turns away and then returns –
have vanished, never to be seen again,
except in memory and vague,
things seductive as the cave of dreams,
its gate of ivory,
beautiful, threatening,
magical, mysterious,
darker and deeper
than the realm of normal consciousness and day.

IV

And in her bed at night,
beneath the patterned quilt, she glances
at the radiator that knocks,
the curtain that moves oh ever so slightly,
the floor that creaks when no one walks it.
And she wonders whether
objects that seem to be lifeless
might not in fact be animate,

like voices heard
in the ringing of the steeple bells,
forbidden words repeated in their clang.

V

The child removes
the violet lampshade from the lamp,
holds her hand before the dazzling bulb,
extends and spreads her fingers,
sees – enclosed within the rosy flesh –
the silhouette of slender, darker bones,
perceives her skeletal mortality:
a nameless, wordless feeling,
evident perhaps
only in the slightest alteration
of the features
in her rapt, unsmiling face.

The laugh

To the quietly observing child—
in that sudden violent burst of laughter,
unexpected, persisting, and excessive,
outrageous as a foaming fit of madness,
in that looming form before her:
the horror.

The head thrown back
like the eager, whiskered seal
poised on the rocks at the old aquarium,
about to catch a flung fish,
but here the slitted human eyes
tearing in that bestial face,
near crimson now,
as peculiar gasping sounds erupt
from the swollen, swaying belly
through the gaping mouth,
until
the misshapen, contorted face of the laugher
is slowly, carefully corrected
to the calmed and sociable smile,
before that quietly observing child.

Lone Ranger

A boy in a black Lone Ranger mask,
beneath a big-brimmed cowboy hat,
who looks away, although
he points his silver pistol
directly at you, the viewer;
and a girl in a white dress
and long brown curls,
who daintily holds up
the corners of her skirt,
as she curtsies
and gazes at the camera,
questioning.

And where is that other child
who rode no-hands
through the streets of your childhood,
but glimpsed only in passing,
on a blue bicycle?

By day the clatter of helicopters
over field and forest,
by night the trembling beams of flashlights
piercing the underbrush,
searching for the lost child.

Metamorphosis

My children have never seen me
in my green rubber protective suit,
my green rubber boots and gloves,
my eyes hidden behind my gasmask
with its massive bulging goggles
and bestial projecting snout,
like the proboscis of some monstrous insect,
or a 1938 vision of a Martian,
as, beneath a scalding sun,
a rubber hose sprays ice-cold water over me,
 while my boots fill with my own sweat,
and I waddle toward those ominous metal cylinders
with my heavy-gloved hands flapping and flailing,
like the rudimentary wings of a randy penguin.

For I have become the crayon drawing
that my six-year daughter made for me
as a present on my thirtieth birthday,
a drawing of my head beside a lamp
heaps of papers and piles of books before me,
an ancient purple pen between my fingers,
furrows on my brow, a frown on my face,
and beneath my huge and glaring glasses -
my eyes unseen.

Thus on this high summer night I must face
the frantic circular dance and flutter
of pallid moths and all those others,
those minute and nameless creatures
that flee the all-encompassing dark
to the lure of the single yellow lamp
that rests upon my littered desk
and shines down on my moving midnight hand.

In solitude and secret then
I set down my ancient purple pen
and read again and yet again
the suicide note of one most dear,
before I quite turn out that luring light
and to the empty room I say goodnight.

For as a swiftly moving hand casts a moving shadow
on the moth beneath it,
and the settled moth casts a settled shadow
on the static table where it rests,
each shadow is consumed in one far greater shadow.

This is what my father told me…

Flight

I

"We gaze from the window of our orange airbus
at the pitching clouds beneath us,
like the melted ruins of the children's once proud snowfort,
and then our buffeted vessel abruptly enters
a new enormous bank of clouds,
and we are totally enveloped
in a swirl again of seeming snow,
as if driven
in a bottomless blizzard.

II

But why am I so fascinated still by human flight…?
There once was a time
when every take off was mythic:
always with the wind,
vertigo on leaving earth,
the tilting landscape,
strings of beaded light below,
masses of darkness,
and brushed by moonlight—
the heaving sea.

Vertigo and the inhuman whine
of the engines straining,
as a child would cry
beneath rcd lights in the dark cabin.

III

Once, seated at the window of a yellow Boeing
droning through the night, my brother and I,
we notice in the darkness there outside
a light that seems to follow us,
mysterious and ever present;
and then we realize this light is part
of our machine, and mounted on the unseen wing,
and that the sky, except for us, is empty.

IV

Now morning descent from blue sky and brilliant sun
above that mountain range of clouds,
their subtle architecture
formed of cream and cotton,
as we fall through layers of heavy mist,
where slanting sunbeams penetrate at times
from gaps in higher banks,
until a tipped and listing landscape
suddenly appears, of patches, checkerboards
of green and brown, thin ribbon roads,
some scattered houses, blacker ponds,
and then the not-so-distant city in its smog.

But also somewhere in the jungles of Iwo Jima,
this I know: there is a fighter pilot
who bears my brother's name,
his skeleton, perhaps is still supported
by the cockpit's khaki web straps,
in a silver plane crashed long ago."

from A Gallery of Introverts

Photograph, 1919

I

My aunt in her soft clinging cloche hat
framing her pretty face,
her big eyes opened wide
beneath the longest lashes, an amber cigarette holder
dangling from between her lipsticked lips,
her flimsy skirt to the bared knee
and the rolled-up stockings,
standing beside my grandmother, her mother,
with her plumed and wide brimmed hat,
a gridded black veil suspended from it,
like a delicate birdcage,
she the captive, yet amused observer,
like a dappled hound
on the back of a fleeing buck.

II

Later my aunt would wear a red fox furpiece
feathery soft the brown pelt,
and the small fox head with snapping jaws
you could open and close with spring and pressure,
as the black eyes glistened
and flashed with the changing light.
But the veils she wore
that flowed down from her flowered hats. –
What did she want to conceal?
Did the red fox know,
remembering Berlin, Vienna, London, Paris?

And when I was in college,
(she a widow now)
I'd take her to the jazz joints on 52nd Street –
to hear old Sidney Bechet, and Teddy Wilson,
and Billy Holiday,
and to the Viennese night clubs on 79th Street –
the Habsburg House, the Viennese Lantern, the Chardas –
where the lights were low and the candles burned,
and the continental singers,
sultry in formal gowns and gloves to their armpits,
their cigarette holders carefully poised,
sitting sometimes on the piano,
legs crossed, exhaling puffs of purple smoke,
talking to us in the audience, in the almost darkness,
in a low and husky voice
with a slightly nasal Viennese accent,
playfully teasing, suggesting a life
far different from my banal and bourgeois existence,
yet not unknown to my quietly smiling aunt,
beneath her veil.

High in the hills of the night...

High in the hills of the night
I follow the peasant girl,
her straw-colored hair,
her swaying hips,
down the dim corridor,
shadows swaying down the walls
from the yellow candle in her hand
that lights her face from below,
as full breasts swell the white blouse,
white wool stockings hug the fullfleshed calves,
and I beside her, eying from the side,
the oaken door, unlocked with heavy iron key,
reveals the ancient bed,
the painted washbowl, white towel across its rim,
the lamp is lit, the smell of kerosene,
a murmured wish for tranquil sleep,
a final flash from glancing eye,
the oaken door is closed.
From the slightly opened casement window now
the sigh of the wind
through the firs on the mountainside,
from the dark, the random
whinny of a horse,

and then the curious pleasure
of sleeping alone in a strange bed.

And then I dream
of when once we,
huddled in a carriage
crossing a stone bridge
in a thunderstorm,
glimpsed in passing,
the shining, foamflecked bodies
of panting horses
beneath the hunters' bloody spurs.

Certain moments…

Certain moments…
like that late afternoon in winter
you, a child, are crouched in the cellar
reading in one of your grandfather's old leather-bound books,
the iron door at the top of the worn wooden stairs ajar,
so that the last sunlight from the southwest
can almost reach your semi-darkness,
when abruptly a black silhouette appears, and crosses
before that opening, partially blotting out your light,
and pauses there for a moment, before moving on,
to leave the light stream once again
down upon you crouched alone in the basement
of that empty house.

And afterwards you foresee another moment
when you are spoken to or questioned by some adult,
and suddenly a silence yawns before you
that you can hear and feel,
an emptiness waiting for your words,
as you pause to savor the coming moment,
curious of the words about to emerge from your own lips
that will shatter that expectant silence.

The last perimeters

I

As you return from years away
in the wider world, you are amazed
at how the streets of childhood here are shrunken.
The avenues that represented once
the ultimate perimeters,
the farthest venture, ominous in gray decay,
forbidden borders, not to be crossed,
seem now so close,
so slight, so trivial.
The home that once was center of existence,
with its limiting periphery,
is now but one more flyspeck
on the map of the mind,
that now contains no single mid-point,
no heartland, no starred capital,
a map that stretches endlessly in all directions,
bordered only by a dim obscurity.

II

In an old photograph of yourself,
in your khaki army uniform,
you observe something
you had never noticed before:
from that distant sunbright day,
apparent now, the black shadow
of an unknown photographer;
perhaps the very same
as the hooded photographer
of your early childhood,
whose face you cannot quite recall,

but whose ominous presence
you still can sense.

III

And now, with eyelids closed, a child once more,
you gaze intently inward
at the knife and scissor grinder
(thick goggles hide his eyes)
with his heavy granite wheel:
as the whetstone whirls and sparks
and the silent children stare,
as the motor of his black and ancient truck
roars and sputters once again,
proceeding slowly and inexorably
down that twilight street,
you wonder where - beyond what last perimeter -
the scissor grinders live
and breed.

The severed hand

I

"It was a time
when all motorcars were black
and airliners silver,
when on afternoons in spring
the sunbeams fell
through elevated tracks
along Third Avenue
to form their gridded shadow patterns
in the streets below,
and dustmotes floated
in shafts of golden light,
as the scent of tawny beer
drifted from the cool barrooms,
from the men in caps and felt fedoras,
each with one foot planted firmly
on the sawdust floor,
the other perched upon the brass bar rail,
as if posing for the mirrors
that faced each other
behind the bar and along the opposite wall
and bore their dwindling images
to all infinity."
[Did my father really talk like that?]

II

"Above the street with a thousand bottlecaps
embedded in its tar,
once again the pink Spaulding must fly.
It was not Nausikaa's wild pitch,
but a solid drive.

In the outfield I
followed the bouncing ball,
ran as fast as I could,
past the last cast-iron manhole cover,
but the ball had rolled
directly down the waiting sewer.

III

I looked down through the heavy iron grate
 and saw below in the dim uncertain light
 that the ball had finally stopped
 in the palm of a severed human hand.
And that was the end of our game for today.
With dusk the streets lights came on,
by themselves.
I took our broomstick bat,
we went."
This is what my father told me, as I recall.

IV

And now a lifetime later,
between the movements of a recorded symphony,
I hear the prophetic coughs of concert listeners
long since departed,
and I think of a man without a hand
applauding at a concert,
and of that roomful of deaf boys
learning how to laugh,
somewhere out there in radioland.

The cave

Those free wild summers of childhood
adventures on sandy, shell strewn beaches,
to the roar of crashing waves
in the glare of the sun or the pallid glow of the moon,
or in the nearly silent, lightless caves of dripping limestone,
there at the very back and base of the brain,
as once again I walk crouched
ever deeper into the mountain cavern
until that jagged point
where I can move only prone and crawling,
crawling on my belly through the darkness,
as my unsteady flashlight,
one able to cast but a dim and wavering beam,
brushes the bright faceted crystals of the walls
and the glint of dripping water droplets;
and then that curious moment –
I hear another sound that is not water,
and far ahead through the groves of stalagmites
I seem to see another light, but faint and floating,
but that is quite impossible, of course,
since I had entered through the only opening.
And then, amidst the darkness of this limestone cavern,
my flashlight suddenly goes out,

and I feel my body fear, damp wool,

and wet rock against my knees and hands,

while in my ears the sound of water droplets

dripping from the unseen ceiling

not far above my head

seem to ring out ever louder

and, absurdly, I listen more closely,

as all my being thus is concentrated

to this single moment, this point of space and time:

no memory, no anticipation;

condensed in that heavy air –

only now.

I am still there.

The return

It tries to return:
even after we have cut down the oaks and elms,
the silver birches, cleared the underbrush,
dug a cellar lined with rock,
pitched walls of stone and fragrant tawny board and shingles
thick enough and sealed toward the howling winter winds,
raised the roof beams high against the rain and storm,
put in our copper pipes and drains and hidden cesspools,
for cooling drink and steaming bath and flush of excrement,
wired sockets, electrical connections for our light,
our lamp against the night,
even after we have burrowed like the eyeless mole,
hammered like that rapid pecker in the forest,
calked and nested like the iridescent grackles –
still it does not yield, but surreptitious
this invader: as beads of sweat it bubbles from the pipes,
as ice it cracks the stone with cold,
as blue-furred mold and mildew coats the dampened walls,
or as spider parachutes from the ceiling beam
and treads daintily on air,
and most minute as silverfish within the walls,
black ants marching implacably beneath the sink,
and then attacking in the crickets' most fanatic chorus,
or as moth about the lamp, while there outside
in the scented dark the zag-winged bat
flutters through the night beneath the trees and eaves.

For we have invaded an alien land,
and now these alien forces return,
and they lay siege to this our castle:

even as we shiver in the damp,
with dry rot and torpid moths in the closets,
yellow-striped and desiccate wasps at the windows,
and listen to the sounds of the forest –
snapping twigs and breaking branches, and certain sounds
uncertain and incomprehensible,
even as we sense the drip and swell and ooze,
the gnawing of the mouse, the dart and scurry,
the trembling of the subtlest antennae, the finest feelers quivering,
even as we peer from our lighted windows
out into the moving night.

Screens

As you sit behind the wire mesh screens of summer
that enclose the wooden porch
with its two twin wood and wicker rocking chairs,
in one of which you rock,
and the world outside is seen but slightly dimmed
through a fine green grid,
you hardly note
that the repeatedly slammed screen door,
with its peculiar snap and bang
as the children would come and go,
intent and resolute,
this door stands silent.
Yet the hour is late now, the sun has set,
and the children have not returned.

You look up suddenly to see
that since your last recollected conscious moment,
sliding imperceptibly,
the slow black minute hand of the clock
has drifted half-way round that circular dial.

As the pale peculiar creatures
that emerge only in the night,
bats and the beings that they prey on,
moths and the countless nameless, minute organisms
that circle the porch light and cling,
yes, they have arrived, unnoticed,
amidst the first yellow-green flashes of the fireflies,
scattered and floating in twilight and shadow.

At first a vague emptiness,
a faint disappointment and hazy unease,
as when something assumed and expected

does not occur;
then echoes in the back of the brain,
like spoken sounds approaching but not quite reaching
meaning.
(Behind your back
the striped and fur-clad caterpillar
has plodded vertical and down
the metal meshes of that screen
till just above your head,
where she pauses.)

And then, like the raucous voice of an unseen parrot
abruptly screaming from its covered cage,
the startled awareness, near to terror.

Thus now you must focus your mind, think clearly,
as one might raise his black binoculars
and hold them to his eye and gaze from the mountain ridge
at a curious flash of color seen on the opposite slope,
while carefully adjusting the lenses,
until the shocking scene becomes quite clear.

On summer nights I hear the cries

On summer nights I hear the cries
of the old women from the Hebrew Home,
calling for their mothers, confused,
entreating in languages
that none here now can speak,
near blind and deaf, and lost in the whirl
of time and remembrance,
and some at times recall, with pleasure and pain,
those now forgotten old-world orchestras,
once heard at spas, hotels, and seaside piers,
salon music, Kurmusik,
Italian overtures and military marches,
Viennese waltzes, operetta favorites,
and sobbing Gypsy violins,
for the sick, the aged, the bored, the lonely, the dying,
taking the waters at hot sulphur springs
and bathing their bodies in mud;
and one recalls especially this:
a young mother in fashionable dress
sitting on a bench against an iron fence,
while a child with her back turned to the music
looks through the bars of that fence
at the curling plume of purple gray smoke
rising from an unseen locomotive
at the far horizon.

Winter night on Central Park West

It was a festive evening, candlelit,
a gathering of aged emigrés,
and I, then young, was dazzled
by their conversation – effervescent,
highly literate, in several languages,
but slightly melancholic,
despite the golden wines of Grinzing,
the sweet and amber wines of Hungary,
as the pianist – discrete, in black –
played softly Wienerlieder, puszta songs,
and melodies from once familiar operettas;
and at times someone would raise her head
to sing along, but softly, briefly.
And I heard fragments of their recollections –
ironic, unsentimental (not altogether) –
of another world, now lost forever.

Then - the hour is late - the parting,
the solemn toning of the great clock.
The heavy overcoats, the furs,
the scarves, the shawls, the woolen hats, berets,
papahas, and visored caps, occasionally
a cane – emerge, before the last embraces,
brushed kisses on both flushed and furrowed cheeks,
the lost, the camps of horror not forgotten.
Finally to step out into a chill winter night
on Central Park West, the fiercest wind from the river,
the black branches in the park swaying,
the roar of darting yellow cabs that pass,
their red tail lights glowing in the New York night,
Our gloved hands raised and waving we compete
with doormen in uniforms and their shriller whistles,
amid traffic, bustle, and the new world,
and I knew then that an era was ending.

Divers

I swim amid this unreal clarity
beneath the surface of the sea,
through glades of kelp and giant sea kale,
undulant green as the green rubber flippers
on my feet.
The strange hum of silence
in my ears,
I float as in a dream
past shadowed rocky clefts
where flocks of golden fish emerge
with great unmoving eyes,
pursue me, calm but curious,
while the quick scurry of claw
stirs clouds of sand
from creature startled
on the ocean floor.

My shadow floats across
the bottom of the sea
detached from me as I myself
from world of sun and surface.

Deeper now
I sight disturbance
of the tranquil waters
and pursue:
air bubbles rising
from forgotten diver
long lost
in massive iron-globed helmet,
leaded shoes.
His features indistinct
behind the gridded glass,
his thick-gloved hands
move to the rhythms

of passing fins and floating ferns.

What message does he signal,
in his heavy armor
through the subterranean jungle,
conquistador preceding me,
this my lost brother?

The dinner party

A single black crow gone flying in the rain,
one fond of enigmas, conundrums, and hieroglyphs,
but seated now at a dinner table -- you:
amidst an atmosphere of curry and heavy boredom,
despite the whimsical singeries on the papered wall,
the images of earnest monkeys in powdered wigs
and ornate bonnets, sipping tea or hunting boar
or sledding gaily on the frozen lake;
while before you on the near-white tablecloth,
one between the colors of eggshell and cream,
rest miniature saucers with golden rims,
each with its four thin slices of a lemon,
arid yellow peel about moist inner flesh,
as your nasal cilia comb the entering air
for other scent, like an insect's delicate antennae
they wave about in search of alien stimuli,
when, from just to the left of you, a certain fragrance,
now in the form of an electrical transmission,
caresses your brain, and your head turns
toward its female source,
and your eye alights upon a slender wrist,
its inward turn, where four fine-branching, pale blue veins
flow downward to the delta of the hand,
but northward disappear in shadow,
there beneath the languid satin of her sleeve,
as the silver tines of her moving fork
glisten in the candlelight.

And now what desires arise,
what questions, tensions, shock,
when two pairs of eyes
have met – and link and lock.

From A Gallery of Introverts

The shrug

Observe the woman standing at the mirror,
as she leans her upper body forward,
so intent to stroke the scarlet lipstick
on her pursed and pouting lips.
And then her face becomes the face of one
who looks about to orient herself,
of one who — realizing now the risk
of too much revelation —
at times might check herself,
leaving certain words unspoken,
hence leaving much unsaid,
like one with eyes directed downward,
who watches carefully each step
as she descends an unfamiliar staircase.

But now you note the moistened tip of her tongue
as it slides so swiftly and efficiently
along the gummed flap of an envelope,
one tinted rose and fragrant:
suddenly you must recall
the hurt of old betrayals,
now, of course, irrelevant,
as she responds to your unspoken words
with a shrug of the hips.

Upon the spiral staircase of farewells...

When from high above,
beneath the swaying lamp,
you lean across the maple banister
to watch a woman silently
descend, past dawn and birds' first cries,
the spiral staircase of farewells,
dissolving in the tempest-spiraled eye –
and then uncertain gestures hers,
and yours confused –
you hesitate,
despite the urge to act,
(as when you watch a wasp
alight upon an infant's eye,
must wait until new flight or cry).

Although the shadows loom
and all is movement,
you then must see
with eyes discriminate,
with eyes distinguishing
between – well let us say –
between the white of eggshell
and the white of table's cloth,
or the white of turning eye
and the white of pointed tooth.
And in this skewered moment
you must judge, decide
both quickly and alone....
upon the spiral staircase of farewells.

Her poems

Her poems are as useless

as those finely carved statues

placed lofty and distant

on inaccessible cathedral spires,

or images left in the darkness

of sealed tomb or buried crypt,

those artifacts to us invisible,

or quite illegible,

to be seen only

by the eye of God.

Her paintings

Her paintings:
like landscapes glimpsed by night
on a stormswept highway
through a rainstreaked windshield
by lightning flash.

The call

That night she had two dreams that she remembered.
In the first she was swimming nude beneath a crescent moon,
as slowly as possible, among the reeds of the lake,
approaching the moment when the white egrets
would arise from the tranquil waters
and burst skyward with a great shudder of wings;
and with that sudden ascent she awakens; confused,
and aware of the late night cognac in the room,
she drifts off again to sleep, to that Mexican village
down its dusty streets to the convent church; within
after glaring sunlight the shock of heavy shadow and cool,
and there at a side altar the glass sarcophagus –
bones dressed in silk and lace, the virgin saint,
her polished skull, her skeletal fingers
adorned with gold and diamond rings, and clutching
the amber beads of an ancient rosary.
Again she wakens, now distraught –
the fleshless face, the clutching fingers still
before her eyes in the dark.

And now an hour before the dawn a woman
rises from her bed, for no apparent reason
refuses to switch on the lamp beside her,

instead in total blackness gropes her way

from room to room, slowly, gingerly,

her arms outstretched before her,

her fingers brushing wall and bookcase, console,

to finally reach the telephone and grasp

its curving surface, cool and comforting,

to lift the smooth receiver to her ear;

and then with wetted fingers of her other hand,

she lightly strokes the dialing keys,

and in the dark those knowing fingers dial

a half-forgotten number, long undialed.

The glove

Conscious always of the eyes of others upon her,
feeling her faded beauty, fading charm,
she gazes now at a pair
of hastily discarded eyeglasses,
laid beside a marble ashtray
with a cigarette still burning
in the smoke of spiritual panic.
For like a fly trapped in a cheesebell,
treading upside down the curving glass,
in dream alone she drinks the undrunk wine.

Between self-delusion and self-doubt,
having missed, she thinks, the Nick of Time,
amid the tension between erotic invitation
and self-concealing retreat,
she is possessed of a fascination
with imaginary secrets,
their impenetrability,
and what we all have overlooked.

Thus often eagerly she will await
the nightly return to the life of the womb,
to the bed with its warmth and darkness.
Senses freed from struggle,
she locks her knees against her heart,
until the morning's birth anew,
flung again from the darkness
into light and risk.
At times to her her life will seem
like the elevator
in that old hotel in Vienna —
a swaying cage of iron
descending through a shaft of darkness.
But rather like a snowstorm
in a sealed glass globe,

shaken over the tiny landscape
submerged in its stale waters —
her recurrent psychic crises.

Beneath her reserve and veil of reticence,
at times, however, the unspoken desire;
as the woman pulls on a glove,
thrusting her hand into its limp receptacle,
she forces each finger to the utmost tip,
until, with one final tug,
the cloth and flesh are snug and flush.

And yet that memory (or perhaps that vision):
she, alone in the night, swims out
ever farther into the placid ocean,
still in her ears the muffled roar
of surf against the distant shore,
amidst the glorious shimmer
of silver moonlight on the sea,
and on her own beautiful body.

In the Everglades

The tail as long as the body,
the lizard with the white stripe
down its beige back,
braced on its slender forelegs
and its more powerful V-bent hind legs,
unblinking eyes at the far sides of its skull,
it leaps, boards the unturning wheel of a bicycle,
remains there, body vertical and downward,
head bent horizontal, peering out, alert,
then with sudden burst
inflates the yellow sac of its throat,
now distended, tight, displaying, near obscene,
while on the bank of this mangrove swamp
amidst the vicious blades of sawgrass,
cicadas, as long as your longest finger,
stare motionless in silent fascination.

She murmurs: "Something just crossed my mind..."
and I, behind my eyes, I see a fly
sashaying across a slice of thickly buttered bread.

But she continues: "I was just a little girl,
washing my hands at a porcelain sink,
 alone in a public bathroom,
completely surrounded by mirrors,
and seeing my own face,
my hands, my body, my self,
in glaring light,
endlessly reflected, repeated
wherever I looked."

I nod, she looks distraught, and wonders aloud
why she's thinking of that.
And then she tells me: "That's not it at all.

It's really the dream, a dream that returns."

And in her dream, she tells me,
a spotted lizard in a painting,
a sumptuous Flemish still life,
bursts from the canvas,
darts along the gilded frame,
and with forked and flicking tongue
leaps at her lap.

And she pauses, with a look like one returned
from a long journey
through the looking glass.

The order we have established here...

In the ditch before your house
where the pipes must go,
the laborers have struck on something,
they are laboring to uncover it,
sweating in the hot midday sun,
shirtless now, in the hot scent of tar
they dig and scrape,
as something peculiar
begins to take its shape.

Within, the remnants of a late breakfast
still on the kitchen table –
two half-rinds of grapefruit,
two sodden teabags, each in its porcelain cup,
a crust of toast, and four cracked eggshells
dappled with bright yellow;
and you observe her, reclining on the sofa now,
listening to those Bach concerti,
as with her fingertips she strokes
the most intimate inner surface of the sea shell,
its smoothest iridescent mother-of-pearl
glistening as if still moist from the sea;
and you think of those days alone
hiking through the Appalachian forest,
where, with a quick sweep of the hand,
you gather up the sweetest blueberries
that grow by the trail, to suck them
swiftly against your thirsty palate.

But then, amidst the sweetness of this hour,
you feel it vaguely –

that feeling of apprehension;
for the order we have established here
is unreliable;

as when one awaits the tropic storm –
the deck chairs taken in, the potted plants,
the boards made fast across the windows,
the bottled water stored, the oil lamps stationed,
and the flashlights ready,
the sky a single vast and graygreen cloud,
the air is strangely still, the birds have gone, but where?
Awaiting the first gusts of wind,
the first patter of the single raindrops
before the violence.

A curious tale

Amid their chatter of Provence,
of exotic foods and finest wines,
their fatuous observations
on the just elapsed day,
as words swarm about
like tropic flies about a carcass –
and then it returns:
that memory
of a curious tale,
a tale told upon a winter night
of snow and distant childhood,
but in its telling interrupted,
broken off without an ending,
so that still today amidst your life
you feel at times before you sleep
a vague dissatisfaction,
a lingering air of incompleteness;
as when you find in the snow
a single shoe
and attempt to construct around it
a narrative.

And yet at the extreme periphery of vision –
a sense of shadow and of movement, for,
of course, surrounding us on every side
but beyond the margins,
just off the edges of this page
is that of which we do not speak
or cannot speak.

And now, perhaps,
you drive a desolate stretch of highway
– no stars, no moon –
the dull hum of the motor,
the greenish glow of the dashboard in the dark,

while far ahead, in the distance,

beyond the ken of your headlights,
immersed in blackness,
a single pair of red taillights
is growing ever smaller.

Someone has come late to the labyrinth...

Someone has come late to the labyrinth,
many centuries after golden-haired Theseus
had already left that arid island,
someone without the crimson thread
spun by Ariadne's milk-white hands;
but the massive walls here are still intact,
though sometimes carpeted green with moss,
though chipped and cracked, with grasses growing from the fissures.

And so he wanders this labyrinth, its ambiguous order,
its winding passages, misleading paths,
deceptive signs, amidst a multitude of choices
that lead to confusion and bewilderment, detours,
wrong ways, dead ends, disappointments, culs de sac,
tangles and surprises, the weary retracing of steps.

In the silence of this labyrinth
the faintest sound disturbs,
perhaps a pebble dislodged by a lizard's sudden scurry,
and yet at times, it seems as if there were
another voice in the maze, somewhere
behind the enormous walls he hears a distant laughter;
amidst uncertainty, hope, and despair
he struggles onward, to reach that mysterious center
where still the ancient minotaur may dwell.

But at the labyrinth's innermost core,
who is truly the minotaur?

At the stroke of midnight in Jerusalem

It is like a painting in a painting: on its easel,
but with its back to us, as the artist gazes,
brush in hand, at the canvas,
its unseen unknown image.

For at the stroke of midnight in Jerusalem,
high noon in Purgatory,
five o'clock on a winter afternoon in New York,
a connoisseur of solitudes and silence
stands before a brass clock
dangling in a haze of blue cigarette smoke
and ponders before the enigma of his empty canvas.

But melting ice cubes
suddenly slide to the bottom
of the empty whisky glass
to rattle amid the silence
and startle.

An abrupt awareness:
for there is a figure standing in the doorway,
against the light, a silhouette,
the sex unclear,
as in an otherwise unambiguous painting
the presence of unexplained shadows.

(Something more is going on here,
something still not being said;
something perhaps beyond articulation.)

Like a word, a name,
said to be on the tip of your tongue,
but not quite released to the light,
still bound to beads of white saliva
and the ruddy buds of taste,

a word, a name, still in the darkness
beneath the tongue of memory,
until one day that tongue will slip
to reveal what till then was hidden.

Thus he waits, beside the clock, before the doorway,
as at a gaming table one might watch
the blurred whirl of the roulette wheel,
listen to the clicks
as they grow ever slower in the silence,
the final few interminable,
and then the very last,
the fatal number clear now, the gasp, the cry.

I could tell…

I could tell of the delights of the old European marketplace—
la place du marché, der Marktplatz, il mercato—
the roofed and wooden stands draped high
with carrots, cabbages, leeks, and parsnips,
plump yellow onions, and those turnips,
pale and tinted purple at their tips,
and then the mingling scents of herbs—
thyme, rosemary, mint, and marjoram,
the faintest parsley beneath the strung white clustered garlic bulbs.

But now the great bloody hunks of fleshmeat hung on hooks,
the carcass parts and dripping viscera,
a pig's rump chopped in two and gutted,
a lung strung up beside a dangling windpipe,
and a freshly skinned oxhead with open eyes
that stare reproachfully at those who pass.

Behind such booths the market women stand,
robust descendants of stubborn, sturdy peasants,
about their heads babushkas, bright red earmuffs,
their cheeks ruddy and wind-raw,
their breath curling from their opened lips,
as they call out in their rural dialect
of fruits and vegetables, their names, their prices.

But what can it mean to utter these words—
mere air ejected from the double lung
to pass through larynx, tongue, and moistened lips;
or this ink, black strokes on a page of white?
What have I truly captured here?

Not the fine molecular structure
of all that fresh, the whirling electrons,
not even the living bodies, their hidden crevices,
the smothered breaking of wind beneath their heavy smocks,
nor their laughing belches,
and not at all what every one of them
would think most real—
the inner life, the so-called soul, the loves,
the desires and the hatreds, fears, frustrations,
the unacknowledged ever-lurking boredom.

And with these words what do I say when I say I say?
For to seek to capture with my words
the contents of a single mind, its flux and flow,
is it not as futile as to try to tell
in letters of a human alphabet
the cry of bird or beast?

After the hubbub of hawkers and hucksters,
the daily din and fracas of the city, the seekers,
in the deserted marketplace
now only the gray cut stones of the pavement remain,
dappled with the last droppings
of the departed cart and carriage horses,
save for a single halted chestnut mare,
her head plunged deep in her leather feedbag,
her eyes downward and intent
above her grinding but invisible jaws.
As, filtered through the clouds, a cluster of slanted sunbeams
abruptly focuses on one final aged streetcleaner,
those rays like the shafts of theater spotlights
seizing one final solitary—circus clown.

Travelers

As now we know,
that greatest traveler, Marco Polo,
never left the harbor of Byzantium,
never journeyed over Himalayan heights
or crossed the Gobi Desert's yellow sands,
but sat in this same smoke-filled harbor café
and listened to the tales of turbaned Persian merchants,
their silks and camels, their travels
to the Khan and far Cathay;
and then at night in dream and fever
he travels far himself,
and fourteen summers later
wakens in a Genovese prison –
the dripping water the scurry of rats, the stench –
and, bound in chains, he tells a fellow prisoner
of his adventures;
who writes it down, when freed transmits it,
scribes transcribe it, spread it far and wide,
to stir the minds of greedy doges,
distant kings and kaisers,
and turbaned Persian merchants
who sit cross-legged, wreathed in smoke,
in this very same café
in the harbor of ancient Byzantium.

Museum peace

At a museum in Münster, Westphalia,
(where the treaty was finally signed
for the end of the Thirty Year's War)
on the earliest independent still life painting
in the history of European art,
by Ludger Tom Ring the Younger,
anno domini 1562,
inscribed on that painted stoneware flower vase,
with its white lilies
and dull red iris blossoms,
in majuscule Roman letters,
the Latin verses:

IN VERBIS
IN HERBIS
ET IN LAPIDIBUS
DEUS

in words
in plants
and in stones
God

The Village Advocate" by an unknown Dutch Master, c. 1600

Arrogant and condescending,
pointed nose, pointed beard, and pointing finger –
the lawyer in his chamber
heaped with legal papers, letters, briefs,
and crumbling documents,
in every corner bundles of forgotten pleas,
upon his desk his quills, his blotting sand, his knife,
and stains of ink spills, laced with parings
from his yellow fingernails, confusion and chaos,
and mountains of paper that threaten
to topple on the scattered sheets
he now peruses.

There is an odor in the room. Or odors.
The peasants. His clients. Their sweat.
Big-bellied women, their wicker baskets filled with eggs,
their unkempt men with unplucked chickens
dangling from their fists,
mud and manure clinging to their boots.
The room is bursting with these bodies –
physical, fleshly, producers of eggs and sperm,
spewers of spittle and feces,
wafters of redolent breath and flatulence,
souls of oats and barley, cabbage and onions,
they grovel now before their advocate.

For the power of the robust body
that must walk each day
behind the steaming ox,
the oak and iron plow,
through stony fields,
that each December must slaughter a hog,
and cut its throat amidst its screams,
and slit its belly,
drain its blood in battered basin —

this force encounters one yet more mysterious —
the power of the written word,
those enigmatic symbols scratched on paper
that suggest a power remote, intangible,
the force that shapes their lives — embodied now
in a foolish man whose spectacles are slipping
down his pointed nose.

The artist Alfred Kubin in an ancient Slavic city

Night and starless sky. I cross the ancient stone bridge, flanked by the enormous limestone bodies of writhing martyred saints, their mouths wide open. Behind the fog rising from the river, total black and silence, except for the echo of my footsteps on the cobblestones. I descend the last steep stairs from the bridge and reach a street, as foul vapors rise from the sewers and mingle with the mist. Only an occasional light in a window far off, up high; other footsteps at times, heard before a body is seen. Beneath a streetlamp, briefly, a shadowy mass, moving always away, into the enveloping darkness. I ask a question of a fleeting form. A reply like a laugh, from a face averted, receding footsteps. By the light of a distant streetlamp, I try to read a street sign, but the letters swim, mean nothing, and then the climb into the murk, a hundred steps, above me only mist, two hundred, endless, a weariness, a pause. Yet in the chill nothing is familiar, still long before the dawn. Somewhere above me lies my destination, a massive crumbling stone house, a gothic archway, and an eagle with two heads. Maria cries.

Gaudy parrots

Amidst the squawks of gaudy parrots

high in the trees,

the endless background chatter

of long-tailed yellow monkeys,

and the quick scamper of lizards

seen but from the corner of the eye,

I, as scientist

must seek out and attend

the last few aging speakers

of a dying language,

one now on the very verge of extinction,

as these final speakers speak

through its most complex and subtle grammar,

certain melodious sentences,

with their haunting sibilant words and phrases,

perhaps never to be heard again.

And likewise I as poet might well venture

to note the small unregistered gestures

of human interaction,

to fix and hold those fleeting moments,

to pluck them from the flux of time,

suspend them in timelessness and light,

and also to recover things half-said,

left floating in the air of this sullen city,

the spoken words still warm from the mouth,

and those quivering just on the tip of the tongue,

halted and unsaid, perhaps

for evermore – silent.

But now, when someone very dear

has slit her wrists

and no words will help,

I attempt to bring alive again her mind

by listening to the music she had loved,

perhaps to find in certain harp arpeggios

in a certain minor theme or oboe phrase,

something in her I had missed, neglected,

or ignored.

Like someone not well rehearsed...

Like someone not well rehearsed
in playing her role on the stage of the city,
amidst the onlookers, bystanders,
and those who bend and cough,
through the most furtive half-seasons
you meander, through whispered digressions
for you do not know the confrontation
of two opposing mirrors in an empty room,
nor what the mirror does in the dark,
nor what occurs
in the unseen world around you,
as the lid descends
to cover your briefly blinded blinking eye,
at that frightful and ever repeated instant
of personal darkness;
nor do you comprehend
the unknown voice
that does not speak
when you answer the telephone
when it rings at the very same hour
every dawn.

Every moment that you think it,
the word "now"
means something different.

Scriptwriter

As when the telephone rings
and someone answers in another room
and you cannot help but listen
to the murmur of her words,
and yet you comprehend nothing,
until the click of returned receiver,
receding footsteps, and the sound of sobbing.

Thus your uncertain horror –
when for the first time
it occurs to you
what your place in the story might be;
and yet the tale goes on,
in which nothing or all
happens at random,
and you hear behind you
occasional muffled coughing,
as you seek to establish
your own distinctive narrative,
not merely play a very minor role
in a film directed by someone else,
with a cast of millions,
for the amusement of a stranger
looking on from the darkness.

The endless task

A bowl of fruit
beside a porcelain bath
from which a hand is reaching.

Lost words, lost candor –
for there is one door in your home
that you have never opened;

for something more is going on,
something still not being said,
subliminal or veiled,
something perhaps beyond explicit formulation –
amidst unnoticed configurations
and hidden networks,
amidst the endless task
of searching for words behind words,
for things behind things,
the child voyeur,
denied for decades
the ultimate glimpse,
her gaze turned inward now,
hands that tremble
as they turn the pages,
an eye seen through a keyhole.

The outpost

The world illumined solely
by a single bulb
swaying from a black cord,
and you stand alone in the night,
winding the clock,
as behind the dunes, dully,
you hear the ocean's roar,
and now the radio bulletins
report of rising tides,
several feet above the normal,
and flood warnings,
as distant lightning
crackles through the airwaves
in time with distant thunder;
while here the steady hiss of rain,
occasional mighty gusts of wind
that flail against the windows.
This solitary house, an outpost
against that swirling gray immensity,
like your own gray brain
against that other gray immensity.

A.R. is in a coma

His studio crammed to the ceiling with papers, paintings, prints, drawings, books, so many books, and clocks that tick and some that do not, and candles, candle stubs sunken in melted wax, gramophone records, forgotten empty whiskey glasses, stashed, half hidden, poised precariously, brown and viscous at the bottom, and junk, a lifetime's detritus, surrounding a slender bed, a chair, a wooden table with a single lamp.

And as he sinks still deeper into coma, a sudden image permeates her brain, a vision of the oldest living creatures, from centuries past, those monstrous clams in the murk beneath the Greenland ice; within their petrifying shells, their ancient flesh, unseeing slime, still pulses, absorbing and secreting — mindless.

And on that table a single whisky glass, empty but for melting ice cubes and colorless dregs, a bright red smudge of lipstick on its rim.
Smoke curls from a cigarette still burning, perched on the rim of the ashtray there, a simple clam shell.

Self- portrait of the artist dreaming

"What is this wolf
that howls at the moon of the mind?"
asks an aging author,
reduced to reading his old notebooks
filled with plans and projects,
with images and apercus,
those fragments of a past now lost,
elusive experiences, driftwood,
and what might have been—
the tenuous, the blurred, the tremulous:
as one might try to prolong
the ecstasy of vertigo,
the dizzying near nausea
of peering down from a great height
at the very edge of a sheer drop,
so long as one felt quite secure
behind an iron barrier—thus he seeks
to complete the partially apprehended,
seeking something hidden,
between the lines
or behind the words,
like cigarette smoke, perfume,
and a sweet breath of alcohol,
something cryptic
that must be there,
voices of the winter night,
voices that lure him
to walk the moonlit ice
of the frozen lake.

Poem on the title of my book Wordglass

Wordglass: words made of glass,
those firm transparent vehicles
to the fluxus of realities behind them,
windows clear and crystalline,
shedding light,
framing and composing
what lies there outside.

Wordglass:
perhaps the goblet filled with words,
the red wine of language,
a cornucopia of sense impressions,
of flavors mellow, dry or sweet,
or subtly blended,
to slide along the budded tongue,
bouquet to draw in through the nostrils
to caress those finest ferns within,
a taste of bubbling intoxication
or the sober chill of ice water.

Word glass:
the mirror's glass,
opacity of silver language,
reflecting outer world,
its color, form, obscurest interpenetrations,
and multiple movements in space and time,
and more, though indirect,
a magic mirror of the inner world,
the unseen realm we think we share,
a mirror in the dark.

Wordglass:
perhaps to word, a verb, imperative,
to word the wordable,
the very vehicle itself,
whether in a wineglass, through a window,
or in the shadowed mirror's depths.
Word, glass.

P.H. in Paris

I had to leave:
as when one seated at the cinema,
distressed by the inanity of the film
that he is watching, rises from his seat
and makes his way along the knees
of those still seated and engrossed beside him,
to the aisle; and there with lowered head –
although the arching silhouette of his skull
must briefly pass across the screen –
he hastens through the darkness to that word
in red electric light – SORTIE.

And thus:
I stand now at this stagnant forest pond,
dimpled with sunlight, tree shadows, and water lilies,
where a blue dragonfly hovers
over its own liquid reflection.
II
For the forbidden grottoes of my childhood
could lure me once again.

I well recall the entrance on the hillside,
through the tangled underbrush,
the vines, half-hidden there, the thorns.
Then through the darkness of the cave
we children, the two of us, would grope and crawl,
our flashlights casting trembling beams before us,
until we reached the largest chamber,
where we could stand erect beside the pool,
to watch its eyeless milk-white salamanders
as they swam in our feeble cones of light,
and above them, the dripping stalactites aglisten,
and we would stand and stare, each time in awe.

And still today I dream that mineral realm
and all that's subterranean and dank,
like the secret life of the plants
in their eternal dark beneath the earth,
the swelling bulbs, the pallid darting tubers,
the writhing clutching roots,
the utmost tip of every root, itself
a tiny sucking mouth.

Earth calls.

Voices
Of asylums for the insane
I

When the Emperor Franz Joseph wrote to the Empress Elizabeth
to ask her what she would like to receive
for her approaching name day, she at once replied:
"a completely equipped insane asylum,"
perhaps one like the old Vienna Madhouse
with its great March Mardi Gras Ball,
where--in revealing and most outrageous costumes—
for a single night
the masked lunatics could dance till dawn;
or one like Bedlam, where aristocratic and amused guests
in their bonnets and hoopskirts, periwigs and silken breeches,
would visit that famous London madhouse
to observe the naked inmates shriek and writhe,
as they rolled on that filthy floor and soiled themselves;
although, of course, the kindly empress could not know
of that distant island Delirios,
off the rocky coast of Southern Anatolia,
where the madmen wait each August
for the horses that come to grind the grain;
and the madmen watch them very closely,
as they swim ashore through waves and surf,
upon their dripping manes as they emerge—
the flecks of foam,
the limp and glistening jelly fish.

II

In memory now you watch a silent woman,
standing, staring straight before her
at something that you cannot see,
as in each tightly clenched fist
she crushes a single white egg,

their brittle shells cracking,
until from between her fingers
the white and yolk begin to seep and drip,
a viscous glossy clinging yellow ooze
falling to the kitchen floor,
as from a clenched but retching mouth.

III

Now if you were to walk
beside a sun-bright autumn lake,
its calm unwrinkled surface
mirror for the gold and russet foliage
along its tranquil shore,
and skyblue at its center,
together with a woman,
ever and exceedingly conscious
of her own breathing,
of the need to suck in air,
of the saliva gathering
within the basin of the mouth,
of the need, the constant urge
to swallow,
who feels her weathered and uncertain face —
like Strindberg's paintings—
to be seen only by firelight
or in a room halfdarkened,
one who hears insistent voices,
one who must live apart,
behind thick walls with windows barred,
where she is supervised and drugged,
where she has known insulin,
ice baths, and electro-shock,
and is permitted such release
and briefest visit
only rarely—
what then would your voice say?

Premonition

Night steps in the empty street,
the sense of one behind me,
the shadow in the garden.
My thought – the unheard shriek
of the gray-furred bat –
groping, probes, returns
with unexplained vibrations –
the source remote
as the ice-blue
heart of the whale.

Two palest yellow moths
settle quivering
on my eyelids.

Look at your own hand...

Look at your own hand,
like an alien creature
strange and incomprehensible
in its coil and clutch,
as on the bottom sand of the sea
the red lobster's monstrous claw;
and then as I begin,
feel the moment's vague tension,
as when two walkers,
who may know each other,
approach each other,
who yet until
the proper distance
is achieved,
do not greet.

Thus learn the musty silence
of a dimly curtained room
late upon a winter afternoon,
as harsh wind drums
against the window panes
of dust and smoke,
of muffled and discordant cries;
within, the sweet smell
of ancient crumbling leather books
of copper hue, or ochre,
an odor of silk,
velvet, perfume,
dust, and withered roses.
A glitter of silver and red
out of the indistinct darkness,
curious shapes in the draperies,
their oddly billowing forms
such that precocious children would clutch
at their strangest swellings,

the rooms' peculiar leer,
like white teeth grinning
in a glass of water.

And now be still and listen,
hear the sand
hissing softly
through the hourglass,
feel in your ear
time's flow,
the tumor
growing in the dark,
and sounds unheard,
insubstantial vaguely ominous thoughts,
like the half-hidden faces
in Persian paintings,
of spirits and demons,
woven into the contours
of rocks and clouds.
For these walls have ears –
curving, color of ivory
tinted pink,
that bend slightly.
Turning toward the slightest sound,
the spiraled ivory funnels,
motile and attentive,
like roses softly swayed
by truant summer breezes,
or like the eyes
of ten-thousand circus watchers
rolling with the rhythm
of the swung trapeze.

Since awareness comes
like the sudden disturbance
when one clears his throat
alone in the dark.

Whether the mind is a river...

Whether the mind is a river
or a river bed,
whether time is an arrow
or an ocean wave,
on this night
I venture forth
into unknown regions.

Longing for a gesture, a register
outside of rhetorical tropes,
but operating with an enigmatic unknown,
an unanalyzable x,
and, of course, both beginning and end
inaccessible,
and between these inaccessible limits
only fragments to be found,
to reveal layers
of indeterminate and shifting messages
that I cannot behold
but asquint
upon a vestige.

As when we overhear
fragments of a conversation –
phrases, words, pieces of meaning,
and we are forced to fill the blanks,
give structure to the random,
construct a frame, a string, a story.
We listen to the modulations,
the inflections and the breaks,
we try to judge the tone of voice,
the veracity and the intent,
to ourselves interpreting,
as from a foreign language;
we evaluate the cough, the laugh, the loudness –

the sources: unknown narrators
telling of persons and places unknown to us,
the unity created from the depths
of our own unknown selves.

Thus floating layers of consciousness
that sometimes intersect or overlap,
or run on, parallel but separate,
amid the fascination of memory,
the half-forgotten and the magic
of the past that lingers
in the dim unconscious,
like whispered words once overheard,
a glimpse in a window
of a winter evening,
or a neglected garden
where ripe red apples
fall in the night, remain unpicked
to lie, to rot. For it is always in the background
that trouble brews.

And then this rustling
in the godforsaken books,
behind the letters
nothing, breath at most,
like the sounds of the sleeper
writhing
in the throes of her dream,
or the unheard sounds
of the subterranean world,
the breath and groan
of granite, coal, and crystal.
(And yet at times, of course,
amidst the words
a sweetness lurks,
like the fragrance of peaches
ripening in a room.)

But Schönfeld limned it well:
a man in a gray broadbrimmed hat
and a yellow cloak,
his back to us
points at the bound and anguished Christ –
as languid thinkers,
leaning, half-nude,
look on, absent, listless, lost.

And now regard
the vacant seat at the banquet,
left for the departed one,
or the one to come –
in honor of the void.

A story of waters

Through the glass of your eyes
you see forms approaching,
dimly,
like carp rising green
from the depths of the fish pond,
vaguely,
as bubbles rise to the surface
and the water clouds,
a memory of waters.

You hold the vodka glass
before the light,
glistening beads of sweat
stippled silver on the sides;
within, the floating lime
seen green and distorted
through prisms of blueveined ice.

As far away in space and time
the crouching surfer rides
the inward curving rim
of long and shoreward sweep of wave;
balancing precarious
along the glassy slope,
he races horizontal,

always the growing wave,
leaving just behind
the curling lip,
the coming crash;
ever poised above him
roars the trembling wall of water,
tons of green and liquid marble,

crest of foam

he just eludes.

As in the forest she
paints the pond,
the structures of water surfaces,
the arrowing interpenetration of ripples,
the striations
and delicate punctuations
of water droplets in light.

That night,
surrounded by the dark,
aluminium deck chairs scattered
random on the puddled concrete,
as floodlights pour on the deserted pool;
on the shimmering surface
of the water's unreal green,
in lush and tangled strands
floats the head of blackest human hair,
as something vague and pink
dangles, bobs beneath.

And now
you breathe again
the dark fragrance of the pond,
of the lily pods, green algae,
and decaying water plants,
the leech of the summer pond
swollen with your own sweet blood
like a ripe purple grape,
the pond's own Eucharist.

While in the caverns of Kricvenica
pure white salamanders
with atrophied eyes
swim in eternal darkness,
breeding ever white in blackness,

upon the blue,
like scattered roses of the ocean,
jellyfish rock in pink and white;
and in your home,
draining water
in its clockwise whirl
seeks the earth's iron core.

Summer night

I

Flying creatures of the summer night
hurl themselves against the screen
at your opened lamplit window.
The whir and thud
of wing and body,
mindless from the dark,
their search for light –
assault upon your own
illumined solitude.

II

You recollect
the easy sensuality
of bodies in water,
buoyancy and weightlessness,
soft breasts raised and floating free,
all the surface flesh caressed
by alien element,
the tactile skin aware.
How the heat of the lulling sun
permeates the bone and brain;
how walking, flesh swells
beneath the flimsy fabric,
the languid sway of hip and buttock,
till warmth floods the genitals
of reclining bodies,
as they observe,
and beneath their half-closed eyelids
float lassitude and vague desire.

III

While on the wall
a desperate woman
in a painting
beckons for help
from someone far outside the picture.
Within her frame,
why does she point
at something outside the picture?
On the other side –
other gardens, other gods?

IV

Seagulls circled, screamed,
and you were two divers
from the gray rocks
into the gray sea,
seeking darkness and the depths,
your white bodies briefly flashing,
side by side in the sun,
till you cut the cool surface,
descended deeper,
and but one emerged.

V

As in a placid seaside home
a shattered ship
in an intact bottle,
or in a green bottle
tossed from the sea
an ancient message
that you cannot read:
thus the dream vanishes;
for the memory of that dream
is soon swallowed up

like a seaside child
caught gasping in the suck
of the green ocean's black maw.

VI

For a brief fragment of a second
the bright image
of the switched-off light
remains fixed in your eyes –
in the dark.

VII

The mirror's black void,
the mirror in the dark,
becomes the mirror of nothing,
the implacable fountain,
in this night of necromancy
and dark magical rites,
like the perpetual night
of the inner earth,
where jewels and metals sleep.
And now the miner, Cyclops,
with the lamp at his brow
descends to the mountain's black core.

Portrait...One who has lived long alone

One who has lived long alone,
but who has avoided the eccentricity
of conversing aloud with himself,
he will at times, with others present,
note with some surprise
his own harsh voice resounding,
like that of a total stranger.

Perhaps like the last gray monk
in that crumbling monastery
on a crag above the gray sea,
long since forgotten by the invading barbarians.

Thus one living long alone
will come to look upon himself
as a foreign creature, an alien,
to be observed from a distance,
coolly, remotely, skeptically;
unlike the unwitting, arrogance of the confident,
the dreadful egotism of the shy,
the self-conscious, the embarrassed,
that he once embodied,
with half a sense that all displayed emotion
is artifice played before the audience of the world,
ces gens qui passent, or too,
for the most private theater of the self.

Hence, at times, wrenched in the night
with surfeit of the self,
he will rise from his bed,
rip off his mask,
stare at the painful mirror
straight and long,
at the mask beneath.

But it is, of course, too late to turn back now,
as with the peculiar sounds erupting from the engine
and quite abnormal flame, your troubled aircraft
has passed already that imaginary point
in mid-Atlantic, equidistant
from the two far antipodal shores —
that point of no return.

His imagined sentimental last poem

As I now look back
on so many pasts
that once were futures
at a time when my goodbyes
exceed by far my greetings,
I must take my leave
of cities that I have loved,
where I have loved,
that I will never visit again,
like beloved books well read in childhood,
with marbled paper within their covers
and old steel engravings of magical scenes,
books that I will never read again.
Yet even as we possess,
we feel the loss,
and only in the loss
do we truly understand
what we possessed,
and all that I must leave unsaid
upon this quiet night before departure.

Thus now I shall conclude
like that youthful actor
who appears upon the Jacobean stage
only after the drama is ended
and the curtain down,
to speak his rhyming verses,
his witty and yet melancholic epilogue,
and to perform one final graceful sweeping bow,
as he begs forbearance of his audience,
those in the semi-darkness beyond the footlights,
and bids adieu.

Robert Kramer, born in New York City, is a widely published playwright, critic, poet, and translator of European literature. Nominated for a Pushcart Prize in both Poetry and Criticism, he is a winner of the 2016 Absoloose National Poetry Contest. He formerly served as Director of International Studies at Manhattan College.

Bio Photography by: Robert Presutt
Cover Design by: Kim Görannson and Allan Harold Rex
Text Layout: James Browning Kepple   UB2018

↓ *underground* books ↓ *1*

Veer _ Robert **Kramer**
printed in NYC 2018
ISBN: 978-1-7322097-0-1
Copyright © 2018 Robert Kramer
www.undergroundbooks.org

www.ingramcontent.com/pod-product-compliance
Lightning Source LLC
LaVergne TN
LVHW091228080426
835509LV00009B/1213